Puerto Princesa

Travel Guide

2024

Wanderlust unleashed : unveiling hidden gems and inspiring adventure .

Nancy wright

Puerto Princesa Travel

Table of content

Introduction

Welcome to Puerto Princesa

Welcome, individual voyagers, to the captivating heaven of Puerto Princesa! Settled on the Palawan archipelago in the Philippines, this city coaxes with great enthusiasm, welcoming you to investigate its fortunes and relax in the magnificence of its regular marvels.

1.1 Embracing Wanderlust

- As you set foot in Puerto Princesa, you set out on an excursion that rises above the common. The air is thick with the fragrance of tropical blossoms, and the warm hug of the sun invites you to an existence where experience and quietness coincide. This destination promises a variety of experiences to please every traveler, from the bustling city center to the tranquil suburbs.

Unveiling Hidden Gems

- Past the very much trampled ways lie unlikely treasures ready to be found. Picture immaculate sea shores with sands like powdered sugar, secret bays where completely clear waters lap against immaculate shores, and thick wildernesses murmuring stories of unseen fauna. Puerto Princesa isn't only an objective; It's a journey into the depths of the unknown.

Embrace the adventure of uncovering nature's tricks of the trade. Puerto Princesa has something secret for everyone, whether you're a risk-taker or a laid-back traveler. Plan to be enraptured by the charm of spots immaculate by the hands of time, where each step feels like an excursion into a storybook ready to be composed.

Embracing Wanderlust

Envision a world underneath the surface, where limestone ponders cut through the earth. The Puerto Princesa Underground River, which is listed as a UNESCO World Heritage Site, is an example of how well nature can build structures. Float through its underground sections, decorated with dazzling developments that reverberate the murmurs of hundreds of years.

Adventure into the core of Ugong Rock, a geographical show-stopper asking to be won. For the daring spirits, a zip line anticipates its culmination, offering a higher perspective of the lavish scenes beneath. Amid nature's grandeur, it is a symphony of exhilaration, a dance with the winds.

Concealed in the folds of the scene are the amazingly confined Nagtabon Ocean side and the enchanted Mystery Tidal pond. Time seems to stand still here, and peace is omnipresent. Feel the delicate hug of the sand, pay attention to the tune of delicate waves, and let the enchantment of this secret anteroom weave its spell on you.

Puerto Princesa isn't simply an objective; it's an odyssey into the exceptional. Thus, dear explorer, prepare your faculties for a submersion into the core of a deep craving for something new. The undiscovered treasures are waiting for you to discover them, promising a rich tapestry of experiences that will forever be etched in your memories.

Exploring Puerto Princesa

As we step into the core of Puerto Princesa, let the cityscape unfurl before your eyes — a many-sided woven artwork of wonders ready to be investigated. From its energetic roads to its social jewels and culinary fortunes, this objective is a tangible blowout for the gutsy voyager.

Cityscape Wonders

Puerto Princesa's metropolitan scene is a mix of present-day essentialness and tropical appeal. Begin your investigation at the exuberant Rizal Road, where the beat of the city beats most grounded. You'll find a mix of local shops, bustling markets, and lively street vendors selling a wide range of brightly colored souvenirs and local delicacies here.

Wonder about the memorable Impeccable Origination Basilica, a guide of Spanish pilgrim engineering that stands as a demonstration of the city's rich legacy. Meander through Square Cuartel, a piercing sign of wartime history, where the remainders of an old post murmur stories of versatility.

The Mitra's Ranch viewpoint provides a panoramic view of the cityscape of Puerto Princesa against a backdrop of rolling hills for nature lovers. You'll see a city that effortlessly strikes a balance between tradition and advancement as the sun sinks below the horizon, painting the sky with warm hues.

Cultural Marvels

Submerge yourself in the social wealth of Puerto Princesa, where customs are commended and stories are told through craftsmanship and legacy. The Palawan Legacy Center is a social shelter, lodging curios that narrate the island's energetic history. Draw in with local people and participate in the vivid merriments that grandstand the powerful socially woven artwork of the Palawan public.

No investigation is finished without a visit to the Palawan Gallery, a mother lode of relics and displays that wind around together the story of the locale's native networks. From complicatedly woven materials to old devices, each show is a part of the unfurling story of Palawan's past.

Go for a walk through the Baywalk, a picturesque promenade that wakes up at night with neighborhood food slows down and live exhibitions. As you take in the pulsating rhythm of Puerto Princesa's cultural heartbeat, let the sea breeze accompany you.

Culinary Delights

Puerto Princesa is more than just an eye-opening experience for the palate. Take a culinary journey that demonstrates the variety of Palawan's flavors. Start your gastronomic excursion at Kinabuch's Pub and Eatery, a neighborhood most loved where new fish and barbecued delights become the dominant focal point. The feeling is vivacious, and the menu is an orchestra of exquisite joys.

For those looking for a sample of credible Palawan cooking, KaLui Eatery offers a tangible encounter like no other. The menu, which is served in a traditional Filipino house decorated with local art, combines tropical and fresh seafood to entice you with every bite.

Furthermore, we should not neglect Bread Cook's Slope, an unusual safe house where prepared treats and cakes rule. Go for a relaxed walk through the themed gardens, enjoy sweet pleasures, and relish the kinds of Palawan typified in each cake.

In Puerto Princesa, each feast is a festival of the island's abundance. From customary Filipino passage to worldwide combination, the city's culinary scene takes special care of all preferences, guaranteeing that each chomp is an excursion into Palawan's different and luscious contributions.

As you investigate the cityscape, dive into social wonders, and enjoy culinary joys, Puerto Princesa uncovers itself as an objective that rises above the conventional — where each corner recounts a story and each flavor makes a permanent imprint on your excursion. As a result, as a fellow traveler, embark on this captivating adventure and let the wonders of Puerto Princesa unfold before you.

Day Trips

Welcome, explorers! Today, we leave on an excursion past the city's furthest reaches of Puerto Princesa, investigating the charming scenes that make Palawan a safe house for joyriders looking for both serenity and rush.

Island Escapes

Our most memorable stop takes us to the royal gems of Puerto Princesa — its unblemished islands. Imagine yourself on a boat, tenderly floating over the turquoise waters, encompassed by islets that appear to be straight out of a postcard.

Our entry point to this aquatic haven is Honda Bay. Set against a background of lavish vegetation, Honda Cove flaunts completely clear waters overflowing with marine life. Nemo and his friends play hide-and-seek in the vibrant coral gardens below, so don your snorkeling gear and take in the sights. The "lulubog lilitaw" (sink and rise) sandbar of Luli Island offers a surreal experience as the tide reveals and hides this natural wonder.

Then, we sail to **Cowrie Island**, a sanctuary for water devotees. Plunge into the cerulean waters for a reviving swim, or essentially lounge in the sun on the fine white sands. Try the island's water sports, such as banana boat rides and snorkeling adventures, for a little extra excitement.

Our island venture wouldn't be finished without a visit to **Starfish Island**, suitably named for its wealth of lively starfish. These echinoderms can be found dotting the seabed along the shoreline, forming a mesmerizing constellation underwater.

Jungle Adventures

Presently, we should change from the water domain to the core of Puerto Princesa's lavish wilderness — a sanctuary for daredevils and nature sweethearts.

Our wilderness experience starts at **Puerto Princesa Underground Waterway Public Park**, a UNESCO World Legacy Site and one of the New Seven Marvels of Nature. Voyage along the underground stream, wondering about the basilica-like loads enhanced with staggering tapered rock and stalagmite arrangements. As you explore the winding streams, look out for the recreation area's different untamed life, from screen reptiles to fun-loving monkeys.

For those hankering a seriously elating encounter, dare to **Sabang X Zipline and Experience Park**. Rise above the treetops on a zipline, taking in all-encompassing perspectives on the rich scene and the shining ocean beneath. The surge of wind against your face adds rush to this wilderness venture.

Ugong Rock Adventures entices the daring spirits. Climb the limestone development, overcoming its hole and arriving at the culmination for a stunning perspective on the encompassing open country. Assuming that you're up for an adrenaline kick, take the invigorating zipline plunge, making this wilderness journey a memorable undertaking.

Coastal Treasures

Our road trip odyssey closes with an endeavor along Puerto Princesa's charming shore, where nature's fortunes are disclosed with each wave.

Start your seaside investigation at **Nagtabon Beach**, an unexpected, yet invaluable treasure known for its brilliant sands and tranquil mood. Loosen up under the shade of coconut trees, take a dunk in the delicate waves, or partake in the quietness of this detached heaven.

As the sun starts its plummet, we head to the supernatural **Secret Lagoon**. Open exclusively by boat, this secret inlet offers a dreamlike encounter as you explore through a thin entry, uncovering a disconnected tidal pond embraced by transcending limestone precipices. The harmony and disengagement make it an optimal spot for reflection and enthusiasm for nature's miracles.

Close our waterfront process at **Baker's Hill**, in addition to a baked good shelter, yet a beautiful perspective sitting above Puerto Princesa Straight. Watch the sky paint tints of orange and pink as the day says goodbye, projecting a warm sparkle over the narrows and the city past.

On a solitary day, we investigated the islands, dove into the wilderness, and delighted in seaside ponders. Puerto Princesa's road trip treasures are a demonstration of the variety of encounters this tropical heaven offers, guaranteeing that each traveler tracks down their cut of heaven in Palawan's hug. Therefore, dear explorers, as the day draws to a close, allow the memories of these day-trip wonders to linger, and may your experience in Puerto Princesa be etched in the pages of your travel memoirs.

Unveiling Hidden Gems

Good tidings, individual pioneers! Today, we begin a thrilling journey to discover Puerto Princesa's off-the-beaten-path treasures. Prepare for a journey into secret sea shores, captivating caverns, and the entrancing embroidery of nature that anticipates the people who look for the unprecedented.

Secret Beaches

Our journey starts with the charm of Puerto Princesa's mystery sea shores — unseen safe havens where the sands are delicate, the waters completely clear, and serenity rules.

Imagine stepping foot on the pristine coastline of **Nacpan Beach**, a secluded gem surrounded by coconut trees. As you walk around the fine sands, you'll feel like you've coincidentally found a tropical heaven immaculate by the hands of time. You can take a peaceful break from the bustle of everyday life by wading into the water beneath the gentle waves.

Our process proceeds to **Nagtabon Beach**, a separate sanctuary prestigious for its brilliant sands and easygoing mood. Concealed from the groups, this ocean side is a retreat for those looking for comfort and an association with nature. Take a comfortable swim, loll in the sun, or essentially relish the serene tune of the waves.

Explore Port Barton, a coastal village with undiscovered coves and beaches, further. Here, you'll find immaculate pockets of heaven like **Long Beach**, where the sky-blue waters meet the verdant slopes, making a stunning setting for unwinding and revival.

Enchanting Caves

Our excursion into Puerto Princesa's secret miracles takes a baffling turn as we investigate captivating caverns — an underground world loaded up with stunning developments and immortal magnificence.

Prepare to be mesmerized by the Puerto Princesa Underground River, one of the New Seven Wonders of Nature and a UNESCO World Heritage Site. Take a boat ride through the gloomy passages, where stalactites and stalagmites create a spellbinding display of nature's artistic talent. You will be guided through this underground masterpiece by the distant murmur of the river and the echoes of running water.

For those looking for a more gutsy cavern experience, the **Ugong Rock Cave** calls. Rise through the regular offices of this limestone arrangement, where the play of light and shadows makes a supernatural air.

Arrive at the zenith for an all-encompassing perspective on the encompassing scenes — a demonstration of the amicable concurrence of nature and experience.

We can't fail to remember the mysterious appeal of **Bato Caves**, where limestone arrangements stand as quiet sentinels against the progression of time. An otherworldly retreat for local people, these caverns welcome you to investigate their chambers and interface with the old energy that penetrates these sacrosanct spaces.

Nature's Hidden Tapestry

The final part of our exploration of Puerto Princesa's hidden treasures is a journey into nature's tapestry, a colorful canvas adorned with distinctive plants and animals.

Begin by going to the Palawan Butterfly Ecological Garden and Tribal Village, where the delicate fluttering of colorful butterflies' wings fills the air. Meander through lavish nurseries, finding out about the lifecycle of butterflies and acquiring bits of knowledge into the native networks that call Palawan home.

Our endeavor proceeds to the **Iwahig Firefly Watching River**, where nature's secret scene becomes completely awake under the twilight sky. Skim along the delicate stream, encompassed by mangroves that sparkle with the bioluminescence of fireflies. It's a supernatural encounter, much the same as seeing a brilliant night on The planet.

We visit the Puerto Princesa City Baywalk Park, a haven of peace and greenery, to wrap up our exploration of the natural tapestry. Take a stroll along the baywalk as the sun sets, illuminating the colorful sculptures and flowers that make up this urban oasis. It's an ideal spot to ponder the magnificence of Puerto Princesa's secret fortunes.

As our excursion through Puerto Princesa's unlikely treasures concludes, I genuinely want to believe that you convey the sorcery of these disclosures with you. From secret sea shores and captivating caverns to the multifaceted embroidery of nature, this objective uncovers its fortunes to those with a heart for experience. May the echoes of these hidden wonders beckon you back to Puerto Princesa's embrace until the next time we meet.

Inspiring Adventure

Good tidings, individual swashbucklers! Puerto Princesa coaxes those with a craving for energy, offering a kaleidoscope of exciting encounters that take care of the striking and the fearless. Prepare yourself for an action-packed excursion into the center of this tropical paradise.

Thrill-seekers' Paradise

Our experience starts with a sign of approval for the daredevils, the people who hunger for energy and are anxious to push the limits of investigation.

The Puerto Princesa Zipline and Cable Car Ride is a must-try for thrill seekers. Take off through the air with the breeze in your hair as you cross the treetops, appreciating all-encompassing perspectives on the lavish scenes beneath. Assuming you're feeling especially trying, select the Superman-style zipline, where you'll fly face-first, suspended over the lively shelter.

The "Sabang Mangrove Paddle Boat Tour" is the next activity on our itinerary for thrill-seekers. Explore through the multifaceted streams of the mangrove woodland, where your aide will ably paddle you through passages of vegetation. Watch out for neighborhood untamed life, from kingfishers to screen reptiles, as you submerge yourself in the normal magnificence that characterizes Puerto Princesa.

For the individuals who favor land-based undertakings, the **ATV Experience at Buenavista Viewdeck** is standing by. Fire up your off-road vehicle, leave on an undeniably exhilarating rough terrain and venture through beautiful paths. Feel the surge of the breeze as you overcome the rough landscape, coming to the all-encompassing view of a stunning vista of Puerto Princesa's shoreline.

Eco-Adventures

Our next section unfurls with eco-experiences that thrill as well as encourage a profound association with Puerto Princesa's regular marvels.

Take a trip to the **Irawan Eco Park**, a haven for those who enjoy the outdoors. Speed through the treetops on an outright exhilarating overhang walk suspended high over the ground. You'll have unobstructed views of the park's diverse flora and fauna and the forest that surrounds it as you cross the hanging bridges.

For a more vivid eco-experience, the **Mangrove Oar Boarding at Sabang River** offers a one-of-a-kind point of view. Stand on a paddleboard and explore the peaceful waters of Sabang Waterway, encompassed by mangrove woods. It's a peaceful yet stimulating experience, permitting you to see the value in the sensitive equilibrium of nature in this seaside biological system.

A genuine eco-experience wouldn't be finished without a visit to the **Puerto Princesa Underground Stream Public Park**. Join a directed climb through the rich paths that lead to the underground stream entrance. As you make your way to the underground wonder that is waiting for you, take in the diverse wildlife, which includes a variety of bird species as well as the elusive Palawan peacock-pheasant.

Aerial Perspectives

Our experience rises higher than ever as we investigate Puerto Princesa from an elevated perspective, offering a viewpoint that adds a layer of wonder to this tropical jungle gym.

We should start with an exhilarating **Helicopter Island Bouncing Tour**. Take off over the purplish blue waters, jumping starting with one island and then onto the next, each with its interesting appeal. Wonder about the complex coral developments, spot marine life from a higher place, and witness the stunning differentiation of emerald-green islands against the dark blue ocean.

The Parasailing Experience at Honda Bay is a must-try for daredevils seeking the ultimate aerial adventure. Feel the rush as you rise high up, fastened to a parachute, and pulled by a speedboat. The perspective on Honda Straight and its encompassing islands from this vantage point is out and out fabulous.

As our experience arrives at its apex, consider the stunning **Hot Air Inflatable Ride** over Puerto Princesa. Float calmly over the scene, where the cityscape mixes with the normal excellence of Palawan. Capture the sunrise or sunset, which will transform the sky into a canvas of warm hues that reflect Puerto Princesa's tranquility and beauty.

All things being equal, may this experience-filled venture through Puerto Princesa light the flash of daredevils, eco-globe-trotters, and flying devotees the same. From the levels of ziplines to the profundities of mangrove waterways, this tropical heaven welcomes you to encounter the remarkable. Thus, individual swashbucklers, let your soul take off as you uncover the rush, eco-miracles, and elevated points of view that make Puerto Princesa a jungle gym for the trying and the gutsy.

Top Attractions

Good tidings, individual adventurers! Today, we disentangle the embroidered artwork of Puerto Princesa's most enamoring treasures — top attractions coax voyagers from all over. Go along with me on an excursion through the exceptional as we dig into the wonders of the Puerto Princesa Underground Stream, the charming Honda Inlet, and the remarkable experiences with natural life that characterize this tropical heaven.

Puerto Princesa Underground River

Our most memorable stop is the crown gem of Puerto Princesa — the incredible **Puerto Princesa Underground River**. Prepare yourself for an undertaking into the underground domain, where nature's glory unfurls in an entrancing presentation of limestone developments and secret loads.

Board a boat at Sabang Oceanside, and let the gifted boatmen guide you through the spiritualist waters of the underground waterway. As you float into obscurity, be ready to be captivated by the repeating hints of dribbling water and the sensational play of light and shadow that enlightens the enormous spaces.

The cavern is adorned with fantastical shapes and silhouettes created by stalactites and stalagmites. The church-like chambers tell a quiet story of nature's creativity, with names like the "Basilica Room" and the "Corridor of the Mountain Lords." Look out for the inhabitant bats and swiftlets that call this underground asylum home.

Proclaimed as a UNESCO World Legacy Site and one of the New Seven Marvels of Nature, the Puerto Princesa Underground Waterway is a demonstration of the sensitive equilibrium between environments and the sheer brilliance of Earth's geographical miracles.

Honda Bay

Our process proceeds to the waterfront wonder of **Honda Bay**, a mosaic of islands that coaxes flawless sea shores, coral reefs, and greenish-blue waters. Tropical heaven epitomizes the postcard-ideal pictures of Palawan.

First on our island-bouncing venture is **Pambato Reef**, a swimmer's shelter where lively coral nurseries overflow with a kaleidoscope of marine life. Jump into the clear waters and swim close by schools of fish, finding a world underneath the surface that matches the excellence above.

Then, we set forth for **Cowrie Island**, named after the wonderful shells that embellish its shores. The perfect balance of adventure and relaxation can be found at this idyllic retreat. Cowrie Island is a tropical haven that caters to every traveler's desire. You can indulge in water sports, relax on the powdery white sands, or enjoy a sumptuous beachside meal.

Cap off our island-bouncing experience with a visit to **Starfish Island**, where the ocean depths are embellished with a variety of vivid starfish. The shallow waters make it an ideal location for a stroll along the shoreline or a refreshing swim, making it a beachgoer's delight.

Honda Narrows, with its paradisiacal charm, is a demonstration of the immaculate excellence that Puerto Princesa gladly offers to those looking for the sun, ocean, and sand.

Wildlife Encounters

Our last section unfurls in the hug of Puerto Princesa's rich biodiversity — a grandstand of natural life experiences that carry you eye to eye with the miracles of the collective of animals.

Start your natural life experience at the **Puerto Princesa City Baywalk Park**, where local people frequently accumulate and the occupants screen reptiles languidly loll in the sun. Go for a relaxed walk along the baywalk as the sun sets, causing a beautiful situation against the scenery of the city and the cove.

For a more vivid natural life experience, the **Palawan Natural Life Salvage and Preservation Center** is standing by. Home to the Philippine crocodile, the middle assumes an essential part in the protection of jeopardized species. Wonder about these ancient reptiles as they relax in the sun or take a direct visit to find out about the middle's endeavors in natural life protection.

Our process extends with a visit to the **Irawan Eco Park**, a shelter for birdwatchers. Leave on a direct visit through the forested paths, where you can recognize different bird species, including the Palawan peacock-fowl, making it a birder's heaven.

No untamed life experience is finished without an outing to the **Estrella Falls**, a characteristic miracle encompassed by lavish vegetation. Stand by listening to the orchestra of birdsong as you investigate the region, and if you're fortunate, you could get a brief look at the lively plumage of occupant birds.

As our investigation of Puerto Princesa's top attractions closes, may the recollections of the Underground Stream's underground ponders, Honda Straight's island ideal world and the untamed life experiences wait in your heart. Puerto Princesa's royal gems welcome you to observe the magnificence of nature in the entirety of its structures, making a permanent imprint on your excursion through this tropical heaven. Once more, until we meet, may your movements be loaded up with amazement and the soul of experience that Puerto Princesa so charitably gives.

Suggested Itineraries

Welcome, dear explorers, to the dynamic domain of Puerto Princesa, where each corner uncovers another story and each second is an undertaking holding back to unfurl. Allow me to be your aide through painstakingly created schedules that guarantee a vivid encounter, be it an end-of-the-week venture, a nature pioneer's enjoyment, or a social drenching into the core of this tropical heaven.

Weekend Escapade

Day 1: A Brief Look at Metropolitan Charms

- Begin your end-of-the-week venture by digging into the core of Puerto Princesa. Start with a comfortable walk around **Rizal Avenue**, where the beat of the city beats most grounded. Investigate neighborhood markets and snatch a sample of Palawan's road food delights. Remember to visit the memorable **Immaculate Origination Cathedral** — a compositional diamond that mirrors the city's rich social legacy.

- For a midday retreat, make a beeline for the **Mitra's Farm Viewdeck**. Revel in all-encompassing perspectives on Puerto Princesa's cityscape against a setting of moving slopes. It's an optimal spot to loosen up and take in the peaceful magnificence that encompasses you.

Day 2: Island Getaway and Dusk Bliss

- Set out on an island-jumping experience to **Honda Bay**. Start your sea-going excursion at **Pambato Reef**, where bright coral nurseries and different marine life anticipate swimmers. Continue toward the tranquil shores of **Cowrie Island** for unwinding, water sports, and a wonderful beachside lunch.

- At night, advance toward the **Puerto Princesa City Baywalk Park**. As the sun sets, partake in the warm gleam of the nightfall sky while going for a comfortable walk along the baywalk. Eat at one of the nearby fish cafés offering new gets and a laid-back climate.

Nature Explorer's Delight

*Day 1: ** Underground Ponders and Wilderness Adventures*

- Start your inclination pilgrim's pleasure with a visit to the notable **Puerto Princesa Underground River**. Investigate the spellbinding underground domain, wondering about the limestone developments and submerging yourself in the peacefulness of this UNESCO World Legacy Site.

- For an evening of wilderness investigation, go to **Ugong Rock Adventures**. Overcome the limestone arrangement, zipline across lavish scenes, and absorb the magnificence of Puerto Princesa's normal marvels. For a thrilling aerial adventure, spend the day at the nearby Sabang X Zipline and Adventure Park.

Day 2: Mangrove Oar Boarding and Cascade Bliss

- Adventure into the tranquil waters of the **Sabang River** with a paddleboarding trip through the mangrove woodlands. Retain the serenity of the environmental factors and spot nearby untamed life as you explore the wandering streams.

- In the early evening, excursion to **Estrella Falls**, an unlikely treasure encompassed by lavish plant life. Take a reviving dunk in the cool waters or loosen up in the normal feeling. It's a nature darling's safe house, offering a tranquil retreat away from the clamor of city life.

Cultural Immersion

Day 1: Heritage Exploration and Local Delights Indulge in Puerto Princesa's rich cultural heritage. Start your day with a visit to the **Palawan Legacy Center**, where relics and displays recount the narrative of Palawan's rich history. Proceed with your investigation at the **Plaza Cuartel**, a verifiable site that takes the stand concerning wartime occasions.

- For a sample of neighborhood culture, enjoy Palawan food at **KaLui Restaurant**. The café offers scrumptious dishes as well as drenches you in the creative mood of a conventional Filipino house decorated with nearby craftsmanship.

Day 2: Craftsman Revelations and Culinary Delights

Set out on a social excursion to **Baker's Hill**, in addition to a baked good safe house yet in addition a grandstand of neighborhood creativity. Investigate themed gardens, find special models, and enjoy sweet treats that mirror the kinds of Palawan.

- Visit the "Iwahig Firefly Watching River" to conclude your cultural immersion. Float along the waterway as the sun sets, seeing the mysterious gleam of fireflies enlightening the mangrove trees. The tranquility and beauty of Puerto Princesa's natural wonders are captured in this surreal experience.

As you leave on these proposed schedules, may every second be a brushstroke in your material of recollections. Puerto Princesa anticipates with great enthusiasm, prepared to wind around stories of experience, normal magnificence, and social wealth into your movement account. Safe voyages, and may your excursion through this tropical heaven be out and out phenomenal.

Charming Villages

Welcome, individual voyagers, to the charming towns that structure the essence of Puerto Princesa. You will discover the essence of local life, the inventiveness of artisans, and the tranquil retreats that capture the tranquility of this tropical paradise in these charming corners. Take a journey with me through these villages, where each one tells its own story about Puerto Princesa.

Tranquil Retreats

Our most memorable stop on this town odyssey carries us to the waterfront sanctuary of **Nagtabon Village**. Settled along the coastline, this peaceful retreat welcomes you to get away from the hurrying around and submerge yourself in the mitigating embrace of nature.

Follow the sand paths to Nagtabon Beach, where the soft crashing of the waves meets the golden sand. Here, time appears to dial back, permitting you to savor the effortlessness of an ocean-side day. Whether you decide to lounge in the sun, take a reviving plunge, or essentially pay attention to the murmurs of the ocean, Nagtabon Town offers a quiet break.

Play beach volleyball with the locals as the sun sets, or gather around a bonfire for an evening of storytelling under the stars. Nagtabon Town, with its unpretentious appeal, guarantees a retreat into the core of beachfront quietness.

Village of Talaudyong: A Riverside Respite

Our process proceeds to the riverside haven of **Talaudyong Village**. Concealed from the city's noise, this town sits along the banks of a delicate waterway, offering relief for those looking for isolation and normal excellence.

The cadence progression of the waterway establishes the vibe for a quiet break. Investigate the town by walking or by bicycle, drenching yourself in the rich scenes that encompass Talaudyong. Explore traditional Filipino homes that are decorated with vibrant flowers. Each house tells the story of a close-knit community that is proud of its heritage.

For a more vivid encounter, settle on a homestay in Talaudyong. Participate in traditional activities, meet the locals, and savor home-cooked meals that highlight Palawan's culinary bounty. It's an opportunity to observe as well as be a piece of the peaceful rhythms of town life.

Local Artisan Hubs

Puerto Princesa Craftsman Town: Where Inventiveness Blooms

Our process accepts an imaginative turn as we show up at the **Puerto Princesa Craftsman Village**, a center point of inventiveness and craftsmanship. Here, nearby craftsmans rejuvenate the spirit of Palawan through their talented hands and creative personalities.

Meander through the studios and studios, where craftsmans create mind-boggling hand-tailored things, from woven containers to customary materials. Draw in with the craftsmen, find out about the innovative flow, and maybe take a stab at making your work of art under their direction.

The Craftsman Town isn't simply a spot to notice; it's a space to interface with the social legacy of Puerto Princesa. Go to studios, where nearby specialists share the privileged insights of their specialties, guaranteeing that each piece conveys a piece of Palawan's creative soul.

Dough puncher's Slope: Unusual Gets a kick out of Every Bite

Our craftsman investigation takes a flavorful transform as we step into **Baker's Hill**, a town that tempts the taste buds with its baked good ability. Something beyond a bread shop, Pastry Specialist's Slope is an unusual safe house where the masterfulness of baking meets the appeal of a themed town.

Investigate gardens enhanced with perky figures and themed structures, making way for a brilliant walk. Enjoy newly prepared treats that range from customary Filipino baked goods to worldwide pleasures. Whether you're enjoying a flavorful empanada or savoring a sweet ensaymada, Pastry Specialist's Slope guarantees that each nibble is a culinary show-stopper.

Cul-de-sac Charms

Irawan: An Unlikely Treasure in the Hills

Our last stop on this town investigation takes us to the verdant slopes of **Irawan**, an unlikely treasure settled away from the city's buzz. Here, an embroidery of lavish scenes and beguiling networks unfurls, offering a retreat into the hug of nature.

Investigate the town's winding ways, where conventional Filipino houses stand amid nurseries overflowing with tropical blossoms. Irawan isn't simply a town; it's a door to open-air experiences. Take a directed trip across the slopes, where the air is fresh, and the all-encompassing perspectives on Puerto Princesa's scenes unfurl before you.

Draw in with local people, and you'll find that Irawan is a local area glad for its rural legacy. Visit neighborhood ranches, find out about manageable practices, and relish ranch-to-table encounters that exhibit the kinds of Palawan's fruitful grounds.

As our process through enchanting towns closes, may you convey the recollections of Nagtabon's waterfront peacefulness, Talaudyong's riverside serenity, the imaginative soul of the Craftsman Town, the culinary joys of Bread Cook's Slope, and the unlikely treasure that is Irawan. Puerto Princesa's towns are not simply putting; they are solicitations to interface with the spirit of this tropical heaven. Once more, until we meet, may your movements be loaded up with the appeal, innovativeness, and serenity that characterize the towns of Puerto Princesa. Safe ventures, dear pilgrims!

Detailed Exploration

Good tidings, individual adventurers! Go along with me as we leave on an itemized investigation of Puerto Princesa, digging into its verifiable milestones, environmental wonders, and design ponders. Each segment unfurls a special feature of this tropical heaven, uncovering the narratives scratched in its scenes and designs.

Historical Landmarks

Impeccable Origination House of God: A Guide of Faith

- Our excursion through Puerto Princesa's set of experiences starts at the **Immaculate Origination Cathedral**, a respected design that stands as a signal of confidence in the core of the city. Developed in 1872, the

House of Prayer has seen the progression of time, mirroring the strength and dedication of the neighborhood local area.

- A sanctuary with stained glass windows of biblical scenes and religious icons can be entered through its doors. The cathedral's role as a cultural and spiritual pillar for the people of Puerto Princesa adds to its architectural splendor. Go to amass to encounter the glow of the local area and witness the consistent mix of history and commitment.

Square Cuartel: Reverberations of the Past

- Our investigation takes a verifiable turn as we show up at **Plaza Cuartel**, a site that resounds with reverberations of the past. This dismal yet critical milestone gives testimony regarding the lamentable occasions of The Second

Great War, as it filled in as a post for American detainees of war.

- Meander through the square, where remainders of the first designs stand as quiet observers of the versatility of the human soul. The contiguous park gives a tranquil space for reflection, welcoming guests to examine the verifiable meaning of Court Cuartel and honor the people who persevered during a wild period in Puerto Princesa's set of experiences.

Ecological Marvels

Puerto Princesa Subterranean River National Park:

Our environmental odyssey takes us to the crown gem of Puerto Princesa — the **Subterranean Waterway Public Park**. This ecological marvel, one of the New Seven Wonders of Nature and a UNESCO World Heritage Site invites us to investigate the intricate wonders that are concealed within its limestone chambers.

Set out on a boat venture through the underground stream, where tapered rocks and stalagmites make a strange scene. The repeating hints of water beads and the murmurs of the stream guide you through this underground magnum opus. Watch out for the assorted untamed life that occupies the recreation area, from cave-settling swiftlets to screen reptiles lolling on the rocks.

Estrella Falls: Nature's Symphony

Our investigation of natural marvels proceeds to the captivating **Estrella Falls**, an unlikely treasure encompassed by rich plant life. The falls overflow nimbly, making a quiet climate that blends with the ensemble of birdsong and stirring leaves.

Take a reviving dunk in the cool waters or just revel in the peacefulness of this normal safe house. The trip to Estrella Falls reveals Puerto Princesa's dedication to protecting its ecological treasures by providing a haven where locals and tourists alike can commune with nature's pristine splendor.

Architectural Wonders

*Iwahig Firefly Watching River: ***

Our last section of point-by-point investigation unfurls with a design wonder that rises above the traditional — **Iwahig Firefly Watching River**. This location is best known for its bioluminescent fireflies, but it also offers a singular illustration of architecture in harmony with nature.

As the sun sets, board a paddle boat and coast along the stream flanked by mangrove trees. Witness the captivating gleam of fireflies, transforming the environmental factors into a supernatural wonderland. The structural ability lies in the fragile harmony between safeguarding the regular environment and making an ethereal encounter for guests — a demonstration of Puerto Princesa's obligation to feasible the travel industry.

Butterfly Eco Nursery and Ancestral Town: A Shelter of Biodiversity

Our compositional investigation closes at the **Butterfly Eco Nursery and Ancestral Village**, where the designs consistently mix with the rich environmental elements. The delicate balance between ecological preservation and architectural design is demonstrated in this haven for biodiversity.

Meander through gardens embellished with lively blossoms as butterflies vacillate around, making a multicolored showcase of varieties. The town isn't only a vacation destination but a living demonstration of Puerto Princesa's devotion to protecting its natural variety and instructing guests about the significance of ecological stewardship.

As we come to the end of our in-depth investigation, may these architectural wonders, ecological wonders, and historical landmarks leave an indelible impression on your trip to Puerto Princesa. Each site recounts a story, whether through the reverberations of history, the miracles of nature, or the consistent mix of engineering with the climate. Once more, until we meet, may your movements be loaded up with the lavishness of Puerto Princesa's embroidery, and may you convey its accounts in your heart. Safe voyages, individual travelers!

Informative Sections

Welcome, eager travelers! This is your entryway to a seamless Puerto Princesa experience**. Before we set out on the experience that is anticipated in Puerto Princesa, we should dig into the enlightening segments that won't just upgrade your process yet in addition guarantee a consistent and pleasant travel insight. Let's navigate the essentials for your Puerto Princesa stay, including practical travel tips, understanding local etiquette, exploring seasonal highlights, and selecting the ideal accommodation.

Practical Travel Tips

Cash Matters

At the core of reasonableness lies the comprehension of nearby cash. The primary currency in Puerto Princesa is the Philippine

Peso (PHP). Even though big businesses may take credit cards, it's best to bring cash with you, especially if you're going to more remote places.

Ease of Communication Because English is widely spoken in Puerto Princesa, foreign tourists can easily communicate. The locals are welcoming and hospitable, and they will always be ready to help you on your journey.

Transportation Insights

Getting around Puerto Princesa is somewhat clear. Tricycles are a typical method of transport inside the city, while rental vehicles or vans offer adaptability for road trips and investigating farther reaches. Make sure to arrange tricycle passages in advance and settle on a cost to stay away from disarray.

Climate Wisdom

Palawan, where Puerto Princesa is found, encounters heat and humidity. Exploring is more enjoyable during the dry season, which runs from November to April, while the wet season, which runs from June to October, occasionally brings heavy rains. Pack likewise with the lightweight dress, sunscreen, and a downpour coat to be ready for all climate situations.

Local Etiquette

Regard for Customs

Regard for neighborhood customs is vital to an agreeable excursion. While entering a Filipino home or certain foundations, taking off your shoes is standard. Furthermore, a respectful "po" added to sentences while talking with elderly folks or outsiders mirrors a considerate way.

Moderate Dress Code

While Puerto Princesa embraces a casual environment, it's conscious to dress unassumingly while visiting strict destinations or communicating with local people. Covering one's knees and shoulders is a good rule of thumb when in doubt.

Warm Greetings

Filipinos are known for their warm cordiality, and a straightforward "Magandang araw" (Great day) or "Kamusta?" (How are you?) goes quite far in making associations. Try not to be shocked on the off chance that local people participate in well-disposed discussions or proposition a comforting grin — they are truly inviting.

Eco-Friendly Attitude: Take note of the community's dedication to protecting the environment. Numerous regions, including sea shores and nature saves, empower the travel industry. Discard squandering appropriately, support eco-accommodating exercises, and take part in nearby drives to protect the unblemished magnificence of Puerto Princesa.

Seasonal Highlights

Celebration Revelry

Plan your visit around the energetic **Puerto Princesa City Establishment Day** in Walk, a festival set apart by marches, widespread developments, and features of nearby ability. It is an excellent opportunity to experience Puerto Princesa's spirit of community and celebrations.

Turtle Watching Season

From November to Spring, the shores of Puerto Princesa become a settling ground for ocean turtles. Go to **Nagtabon Beach** or other turtle-safe havens to observe these delicate animals laying their eggs — a mysterious and eco-cognizant experience.

Visit Iwahig Firefly Watching River during the dry season, which runs from November to April, for a dazzling spectacle. Journey along the waterway around evening time to observe the charming shine of fireflies enlightening the mangrove trees, making a stunning regular light show.

Mangrove Oar Boarding in Quiet Waters

Investigate the quiet waters of Sabang Waterway for mangrove paddle boarding, particularly during the dry season. Coast through the winding streams, encompassed by rich vegetation and the charming hints of nature — an ideal mix of experience and serenity.

Accommodation Options

Ocean front Bliss

For those looking for oceanfront delight, consider remaining at resorts like **Astoria Palawan** or **Daluyon Ocean Side and Mountain Resort**. These foundations offer an ideal mix of extravagance, staggering perspectives, and direct admittance to the perfect shores of Palawan.

Spending plan Cordial Retreats

Voyagers on a careful spending plan will find solace in guesthouses like **Subli Visitor Cabins** or **Puerto Apartments**, giving reasonable yet comfortable facilities. You can enjoy the charm of the area without breaking the bank with these choices.

Eco-Friendly Escapes Hotels like the Sheridan Beach Resort & Spa prioritize sustainability for eco-conscious travelers.

Settled amid nature, these retreats plan to limit their environmental impression while offering an extravagant departure.

Metropolitan Comfort

Assuming you favor the accommodation of remaining in the downtown area, lodgings like **Canvas Store Hotel** and **Microtel by Wyndham Puerto Princesa** give metropolitan solace. Appreciate current conveniences, simple admittance to neighborhood attractions, and scope of feasting choices.

As we wrap up these useful segments, may you feel greatly prepared for your Puerto Princesa experience. You're ready to embrace Puerto Princesa's beauty, culture, and warmth with these helpful hints, knowledge of local protocol, insight into seasonal highlights, and a variety of lodging options. Safe ventures, and may your process be as improving as the woven artwork of this tropical heaven!

In-Depth Insights

Good tidings, gutsy voyagers! Prepare to explore Puerto Princesa's hidden corners and go beyond the beaten path. In this segment, we'll investigate the charm of spots past the vacationer trails, find the improving experience of interfacing with local people, and embrace maintainable travel rehearses that leave a positive impression on this tropical heaven.

Beyond the Tourist Trails

In the Core of Irawan: A Neighborhood's Perspective

Our most memorable objective past the vacationer trails carry us to the core of **Irawan**, a town that embodies the substance of provincial Palawan. Here, the rich scenes and customary Filipino houses welcome you to step into the everyday rhythms of nearby life.

Take a tour with a guide through Irawan, where you'll travel along winding paths surrounded by colorful plants. Draw in with local people, witness conventional cultivating practices, and gain experiences with the agrarian legacy that supports this local area. Visit neighborhood homes and experience the glow of Filipino neighborliness, offering a brief look into a way of life well established in nature.

For a genuinely vivid encounter, think about taking part in local area exercises or any event, joining a nearby festival on the off chance that your timing adjusts. Irawan reveals a Puerto Princesa that has not been visited by mass tourism, allowing you to appreciate this hidden gem's authenticity.

*Ugong Rock Experiences: Ugong Rock Adventures, an eco-adventure destination that seamlessly blends thrills with nature, is the next stop on our exploration beyond the tourist trails. This site provides a unique perspective on Puerto Princesa's natural wonders and is hidden away from the bustle of the city.

Challenge yourself with a trip to the highest point of **Ugong Rock**, a limestone development that stands as a sentinel of time. The all-encompassing perspectives from the culmination reward your endeavors, giving a stunning vista of the encompassing scenes. The experience doesn't end there — select a zipline drop that permits you to take off over the lavish landscape, adding an adrenaline-energized layer to your investigation.

Ugong Rock Experiences is a demonstration of Puerto Princesa's obligation to the travel industry. The exercises are intended to give satisfaction without compromising the biological honesty of the site, guaranteeing that people in the future can likewise see the value in the normal wonder that unfurls past the very much trampled ways.

Connecting with Locals

Baybay Oceanside Night Market: A Culinary Soiree

To interface with the core of Puerto Princesa, dare to the **Baybay Oceanside Night Market**, an energetic and tasty center point where local people and voyagers merge for a culinary soiree. Situated along the baywalk, this daily market is an embroidery of neighborhood flavors, fragrances, and common soul.

Draw in with the sellers, who are frequently the very individuals creating the delightful dishes in plain view. Test nearby treats, for example, "tamilok" (woodworm), or enjoy newly barbecued fish. As you feast under the stars with the sound of waves behind the scenes, you'll end up submerged in the jovial environment that characterizes Filipino social occasions.

The Baybay Oceanside Night Market isn't just about appreciating acceptable pleasures; it's a potential chance to impart stories to local people, find out about their culinary customs, and maybe even participate in an unconstrained karaoke meeting — a quintessential Filipino distraction.

Homestays in Talaudyong: A Social Embrace

For a more cozy association with the neighborhood lifestyle, consider a homestay in the riverside haven of **Talaudyong Village**. You will have the opportunity to live with a local family and learn about their culture, customs, and home.

Awaken to the hints of the stream and partake in day-to-day exercises, from keeping an eye on the nursery to learning conventional specialties. Participate in discussions with your receiving family, acquiring experiences in their traditions and stories that go past what manuals can offer.

Homestays in Talaudyong give a certifiable social trade as well as contribute straightforwardly to the vocations of neighborhood families. It's a chance to make connections that go beyond your role as a tourist and make you feel like you belong there.

Sustainable Travel Practices

Puerto Princesa Ecological Authorization Gallery: Support in Action

Our excursion into economical travel rehearses carries us to the **Puerto Princesa Natural Implementation Museum**, an extraordinary foundation that supports the travel industry. Situated close to the air terminal, this gallery offers a brief look into the city's endeavors to safeguard its regular fortunes.

Investigate shows itemizing natural protection drives, the feasibility the travel industry rehearses, and the difficulties faced in saving Puerto Princesa's environments. The historical center fills in as a source of inspiration, motivating guests to be aware of their ecological effects and take part in endeavors to safeguard Puerto Princesa's biodiversity.

As voyagers, it is urgent to embrace supportable practices. Regard nature by sticking to assigned trails, discarding waste capably, and supporting eco-accommodating foundations. Contribute to initiatives aimed at preserving the delicate balance of Puerto Princesa's natural wonders or participate in conservation projects led by the community.

Mangrove Paddle Boarding in Sabang: Eco-Accommodating Exploration

One of the best ways of drenching yourself in supportable travel is by taking part in eco-accommodating exercises, and **mangrove paddle boarding in Sabang** embodies this impeccably. Find the magnificence of mangrove biological systems while limiting your environmental effect.

Paddleboarding permits you to explore the unpredictable streams of Sabang Waterway, displaying the sensitive harmony between verdure inside the mangrove woods. It's a tranquil and eco-cognizant method for investigating nature, regarding the environments that add to the biodiversity of Puerto Princesa.

In embracing reasonable travel rehearses you become a steward of the climate, adding to the lifespan of Puerto Princesa's normal miracles for a long time into the future.

As we close our excursion into top-to-bottom bits of knowledge, may these encounters past the vacationer trails, associations with local people, and feasible travel rehearses upgrade your Puerto Princesa experience. You will not only see the beauty of this tropical paradise through these layers, but you will also become an important part of its ongoing story. Safe voyages, cognizant pilgrims, and may Puerto Princesa make a permanent imprint on your heart!

Conclusion

As our Puerto Princesa experience attracts people nearby, now is the ideal time to say an affectionate goodbye to this tropical sanctuary that has uncovered its marvels every step of the way. Let's talk about the memories you've made, the beauty you've seen, and the genuine warmth of Puerto Princesa in this final chapter.

Fond Farewell to Puerto Princesa

As you abandon the shores of Puerto Princesa, pause for a minute to relish the recollections scratched into the scenes and the giggling imparted to local people. The delicate break in the ocean, the dynamic tones of coral nurseries, and the murmuring leaves of the mangrove timberlands — all become pieces of the embroidery that characterizes this heaven.

Bid goodbye to the cityscape that mixes advancement with custom, where the reverberations of history resound in the churches and the flexibility of the past is exemplified in Square Cuartel. The segregated sea shores, stowed-away caverns, and flourishing biological systems will remain engraved to you, welcoming you to convey a piece of Puerto Princesa with you any place your process leads.

However, recall, this goodbye is certainly not one last farewell; it's a commitment of return. Puerto Princesa, with its immortal appeal and steadily welcoming charm, will invite you back at whatever point you long for the hug of its regular marvels and the genuineness of its kin.

Your Next Adventure Beckons

As you set out on the following leg of your excursion, consider the endless potential outcomes that anticipate. Whether it's a re-visitation of natural scenes or an endeavor into strange domains, let the soul of investigation guide you.

Maybe your next experience allures from the transcending pinnacles of far-off mountains or the clamoring markets of colorful urban areas. As you enter the unexplored chapters of your travel narrative, carry the lessons of Puerto Princesa—a commitment to sustainability, an appreciation for local cultures, and a thirst for genuine connections—with you.

Keep in mind that the world is immense, and every objective offers its fortunes. As you put forward, may your movements be loaded up with revelation, wonder, and the very feeling of amazement that Puerto Princesa imparted in your heart.

All things considered, let the recollections of Puerto Princesa be a wellspring of motivation for future excursions. Whether it's the excitement of underground waterway investigation, the peacefulness of stowed-away towns, or the glow of interfacing with local people, these encounters have turned into a piece of your movement inheritance.

Safe ventures, bold travelers, and may your insatiable craving for new experiences keep on directing you toward new skylines. Once more, until we meet, whether it's under the Puerto Princesa sun or the skies of an alternate heaven, may your movements be as rich and satisfying as the recollections you convey with you.

Printed in Great Britain
by Amazon

37245192R00050